Perry, Sue
    Brothers and sisters.–(Celebrations
series)
    1. Brothers and sisters
    I. Title   II. Wildman, Norma   III. Series
    306.8'75   BF723.S43

    ISBN 0–7136–2934–7

Published by A & C Black (Publishers) Ltd
35 Bedford Row
London WC1R4JH

© 1987 Sue Perry and Norma Wildman

Acknowledgments
The authors and publisher would like to thank Indu Patel for her
invaluable help and advice, Queen's Drive Infants' School
Peterborough and especially Denise Carpenter and her class for their
contribution. They would also like to thank Vikesh Bali and his family
for their help and hospitality.

Filmset by August Filmsetting, Haydock, St Helens
Printed in Portugal by Resopal Lda

Brothers and Sisters

Sue Perry and Norma Wildman

A & C Black · London

Today, Ben and two of his friends have a special job to do. They are helping to look after some children at the playgroup in Ben's school.

Ben's brother, Alex, isn't old enough to start school yet, so he comes to the playgroup every week. Ben's baby sister and his mum come too.

Some days they make models with playdough.

Some days they play with the sand.

The baby is too young to play, so she just sits on Mum's knee.

Some of Ben's friends have brothers or sisters in the playgroup. Ben tells them about his baby sister. She likes bouncing on his knee, but sometimes she pulls his hair.

Then Miss Carpenter reads everyone a story. It's about a brother and sister who are not always the best of friends.

'That's just like my sister,' whispers Katy. 'She sometimes gets me into trouble.'

Thomas reads the story again. He's glad he hasn't got any brothers or sisters to spoil his games or wake him up at night.

'Who are you drawing, Thomas?' asks Shehzad. 'It's my cousin,' says Thomas. 'He goes to a different school from me, but we play on the swings together when I stay at Auntie's house.'

Marriam has a big brother who goes to the senior school. She likes going home with him at the end of the day.

6

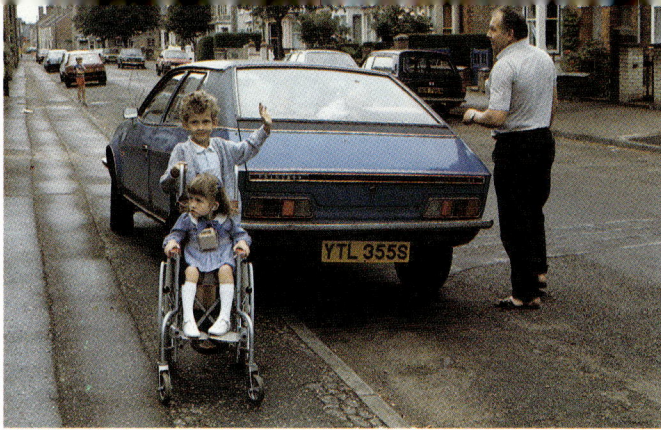

David's sister, Clair, goes to school on the other side of town. David wishes he could ride home in a taxi like she does.

Clair is learning sign language at her school and she's teaching it to David. 'It was a bumpy ride in the taxi today,' she signs.

Jonathan decides to paint a picture of his sister, Clare. She's his twin. She was born seven minutes after him. 'Hmm,' thinks Clare. 'Do I really look like that?'

'I'm painting my baji,' says Shehzad. 'Her name is Mazia.' Miss Carpenter finds out that 'baji' is a name used in Punjabi for an elder sister.

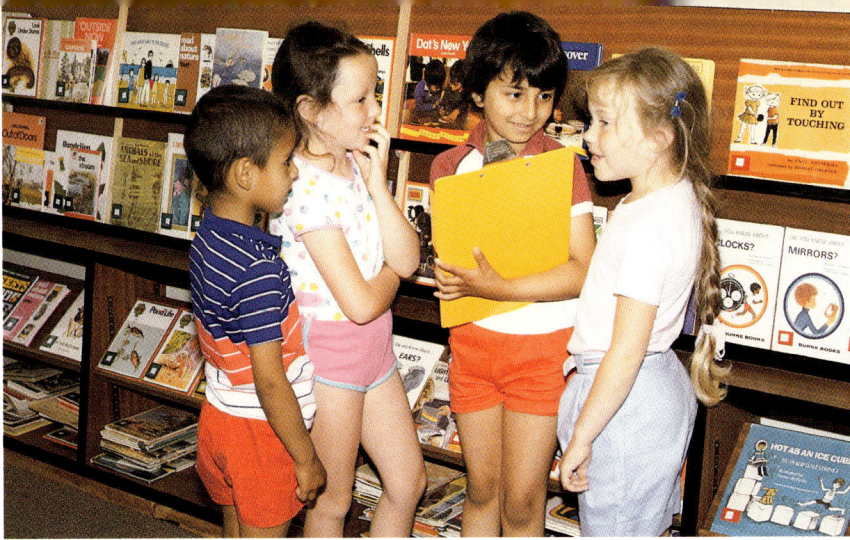

Shehzad decides to ask everyone in the class how many brothers and sisters they have.
He writes down all the answers, and Emma's mum helps to make them into a big graph.

Shaun, Ranjodh and Thomas are playing 'Families'. They look at photographs of brothers and sisters and try to put the right ones together.

'I've put my cousin's photograph in, too,' says Thomas. 'I bet you can't find him.'

Jason has brought in a photograph of his mum's brother, Uncle Ruddy. He lives in Kingston, Jamaica. Jason's mum writes to him every week and sometimes, on special occasions, Uncle Ruddy telephones them.

Emma and Hayley are making a telephone call. They are pretending to phone Emma's sister, Jackie, to wish her a happy birthday. Jackie is eighteen today.

11

Vikesh and Ranjit tell Miss Carpenter about a
special day they have for brothers and sisters.
Vikesh can't explain it very well, but he knows
that his sister ties something around his wrist.

'I wonder if your mum would tell us more
about this?' says Miss Carpenter.

The next day, Vikesh's mum comes to tell the class about the festival of Raksha Bandhan. She shows them how Vikesh's sister, Nisha, will tie a rakhri round his wrist. On that day Vikesh and Nisha will feel especially close to each other.

Vikesh shows Thomas one of the rakhris and tells him about the sweets, called mitthai, which he eats on the day of the festival.

Marriam and Richard want to make their own rakhris. They collect sequins, foil, doyleys and beads to make decorations for the rakhris.

The hardest part is sewing the decorations on to the thread.

Shehzad ties his rakhri on Richard's arm. He remembers that it should go round the right wrist.

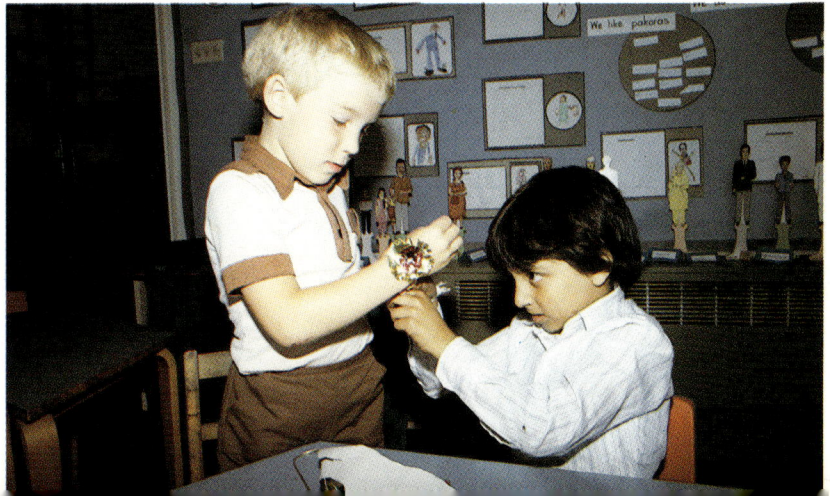

15

Miss Carpenter says that they can go to the shops to buy some of the special sweets for Raksha Bandhan day. Vikesh and his friends choose a box with lots of different mitthai in it.

When they take the mitthai to Mr Karavadra at the counter, Gary shouts 'Hey, Vikesh, have you seen what's hanging on the till?'

Mr Karavadra tells them that the two rakhris on the side of the till were given to him last year by his sisters. He says there is a story that if he keeps the rakhris for a year, they will turn into gold. Rebecca isn't sure if she believes him.

The rest of the class can't wait for the children to get back to school. They all try some of the mitthai. 'This is my favourite,' says Harjinder. 'It's called ladoo. Mummy makes them at home.'

A few days before Raksha Bandhan, Vikesh's mum writes to her brother who lives in Wolverhampton. She sends him a rakhri, some kum kum and rice and, instead of mitthai, she sends him some sugar.

Although her brother won't see her that day, when he wears the rakhri he will think of her.

On Raksha Bandhan day, Vikesh's mum gets up early to prepare everything. She puts out some rice and kum kum which Nisha will press onto Vikesh's forehead as part of the ceremony. She also puts a rakhri and some mitthai on the tray.

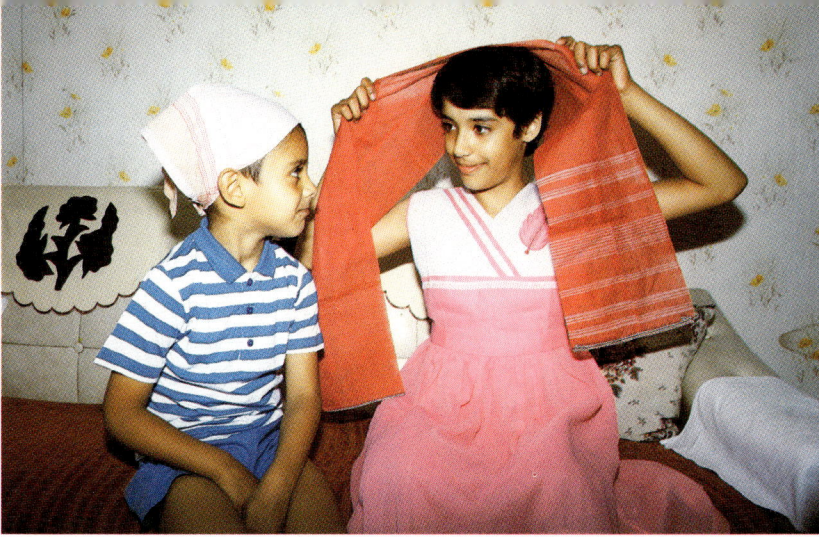

'Now cover your heads you two,' she says.

'Come on Nisha,' says Vikesh. 'I'm ready.' Nisha presses some of the kum kum and some rice onto Vikesh's forehead to make a tilak. She has to wet her thumb to make the rice stick.

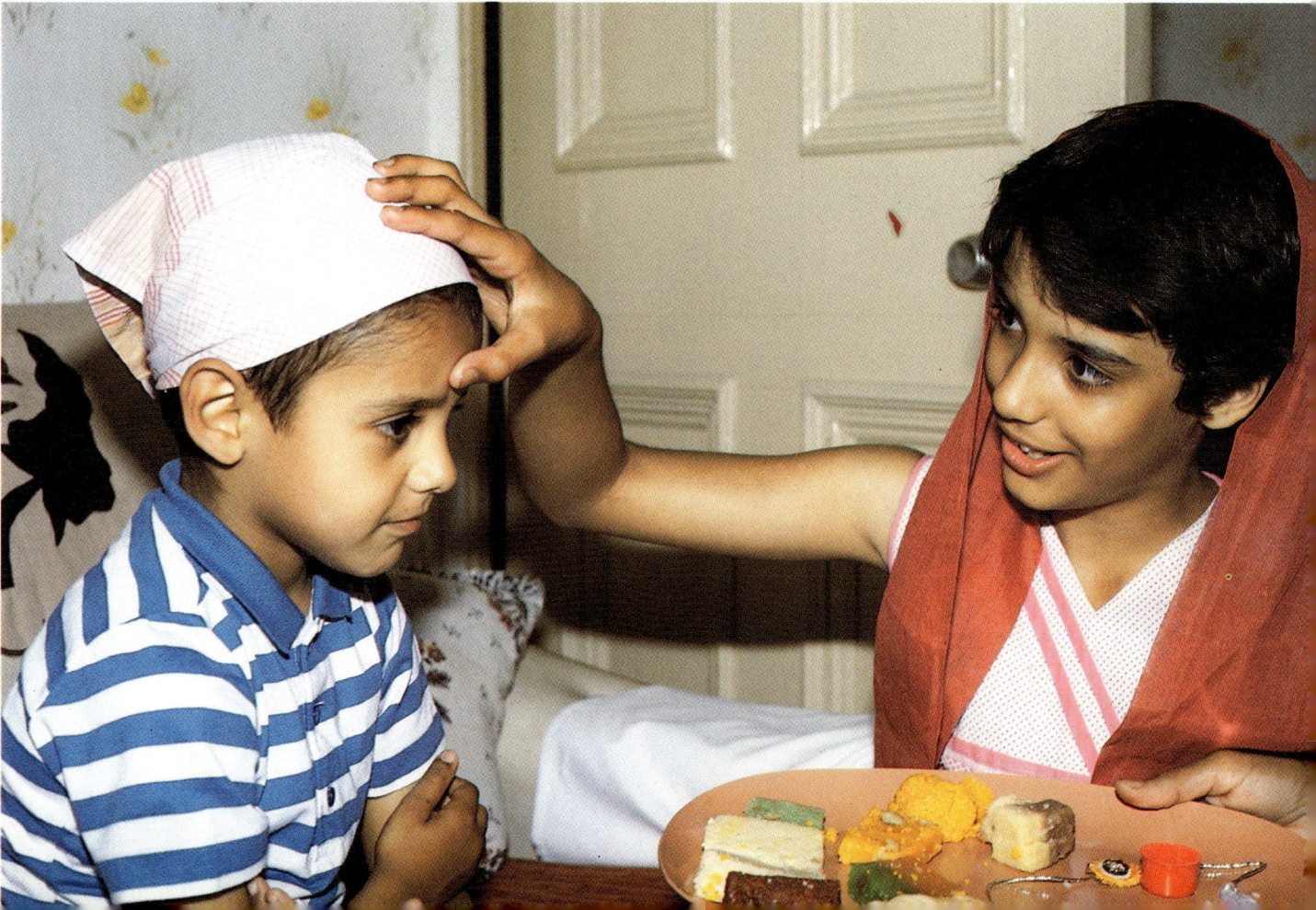

Then Nisha ties the rakhri on Vikesh's wrist. She wants him to wear it for a while, to show how much they love each other.

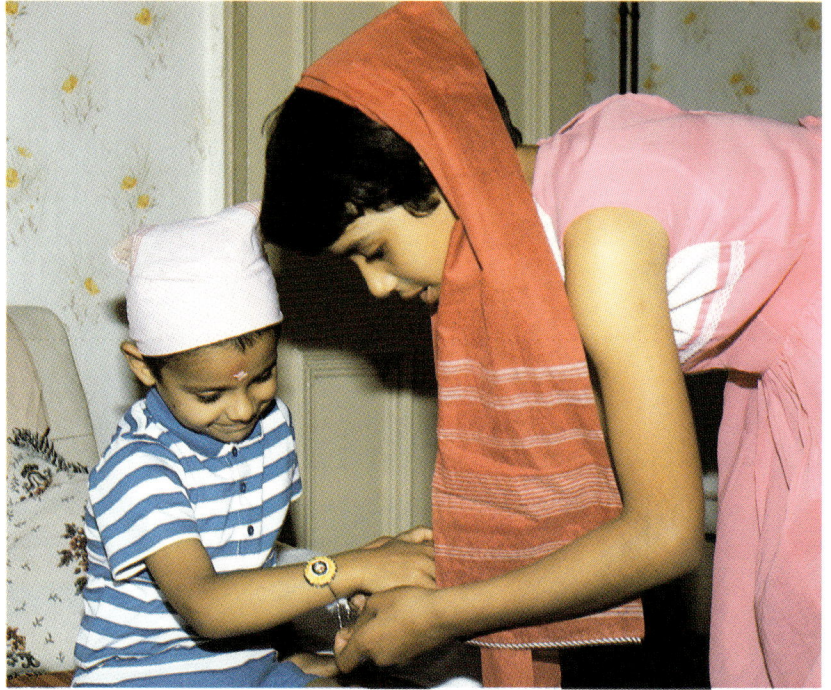

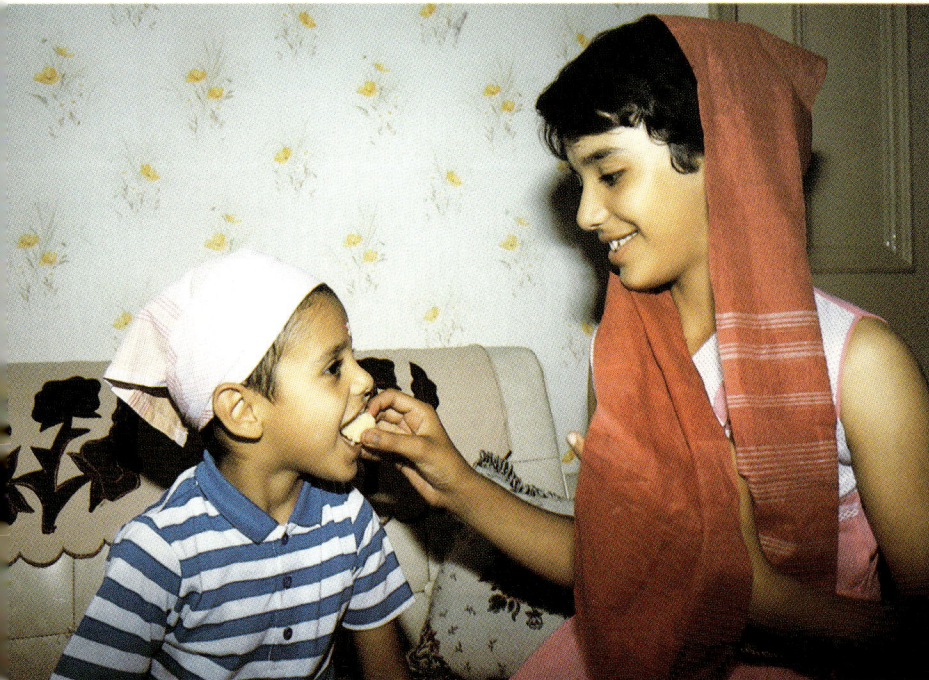

Nisha and Vikesh feed each other with mitthai. 'This is my favourite bit,' thinks Vikesh.

'Take a little bite now,' says Nisha. 'You can eat more later.'

Now it's Vikesh's turn to give Nisha a present. Vikesh's mummy was sent a sari by her brother. Vikesh gives Nisha some money.

'Thanks Vikesh,' says Nisha. 'I'll make sure I buy something nice with this.'

More about Raksha Bandhan

Raksha Bandhan is a festival celebrated by most Hindu and Sikh families. It is a day when people remind themselves of how much they love their family and close friends. The festival takes place in July or August. Rakhris are most often given by sisters to their brothers, but they are also exchanged between other members of the family and close friends. Rakhris can be bought from shops and stalls before the festival and come in lots of different styles and colours.

Families celebrate in many different ways. Some include the lighting of a diva in the ceremony and some may perform aarti (prayers). Some families may cook a milk and vermicelli pudding, often known as sevian, which is eaten during the ceremony. Many families also have a special meal in the evening.

The story of Raksha Bandhan

There are many stories about Raksha Bandhan. Here are two of them. You may be able to find more.

1. The king of the gods, Indra, once lost his heavenly kingdom in a war with Bali, the demon king. Indra's wife, Sacha Devi, was so upset about this that she prayed to Lord Shiva – Creator, Destroyer and Preserver – for help in regaining her husband's kingdom. Lord Shiva was so pleased with Sacha Devi's prayers that he gave her an amulet and told her to fix it around the right wrist of her husband before he went into battle with Bali. Indra's great faith in the amulet helped him to overcome the demon king and so recover his kingdom.

2. One of the Indian states was once ruled by a Muslim King. He was a good and kindly king who loved his people dearly, both Muslim and Hindu. The king had asked his people for help to fight a war against a neighbouring state.

The wife of one of his subjects was very concerned about her husband's safety. She went to the king to ask him to take good care of her husband during the battle. The king promised to watch over him and said that he did not see it as a favour but as a duty because he looked on the woman as his sister.

The wife went home and worried for many days about how the king would remember to keep a watchful eye on her husband in the middle of a fierce battle. Finally she went back to the king and pulled a thread from her sari. She tied it around the king's wrist and said that the thread would continually remind him of his duty to his 'sister'. They made a pledge to look after one another and cherish each other's families.

Glossary

Baji	A Punjabi term of respect used for an elder sister in the family. Some children may use similar terms, such as apa, ben or didi.
Rakhri	A length of thread, often with a decoration attached, that is tied around the wrist on the day of Raksha Bandhan.
Mitthai	(pronounced *mittheye*). A collective term for Indian sweetmeats.
Ladoo	An Indian sweetmeat made from gram flour and ghee, particularly liked by Ganesh, the Hindu god, remover of all obstacles.
Kum kum	A red powder used to make the tilak.
Tilak	A mark made on the forehead as a sign of respect and a blessing.

Things to do

1. Ask at home for a photograph of your brother or sister. Look carefully at the shape of her or his face, eyes, nose and at the colour of her or his hair, skin and eyes and see if you can paint a good likeness. Are you and your brothers and sisters alike?

2. Ask adults in your school if they can bring photographs of themselves and their brothers and sisters. Mix them up and ask your friends to find brothers and sisters.

3. Try to make a block graph showing which children in your class have brothers and sisters. You may have to start with a survey like Shehzad did.

4. Shehzad calls his sister 'baji' in Punjabi. Make a list of as many different ways of saying 'brother' and 'sister' as you can find.

5. Talk with your teacher about all the ways brothers and sisters help each other. Make a list of all the things you do to help your brother or sister and all the things they do to help you.

6. Can you think of other special days when we show people that we are thinking of them?

7. Try making your own rakhri. Make a decoration for the middle and then sew it or stick it on to a thread. You could make the thread from a piece of ribbon or some plaited wool.

8. Can you make a collection of different bracelets and bangles, some of which may be especially important to you, such as the kara (Sikh bangle) or the identification bracelet worn by you or your brother or sister in hospital?

Books for you to read

Gopal and the Temple's Secret, by *Mireille Balero* (Macdonald)
Kikar's Drum, *by Olivia Bennett* (Hamish Hamilton)
The Pain and the Great One, *by Judy Blume* (Heinemann)
Sweet tooth Sunil, *by Joan Solomon* (Hamish Hamilton)
New Baby, *by Judith Baskerville* (A & C Black)

Books for your parents or teachers

The Tinderbox Assembly Book (A & C Black)
Child/Family Relationships (Peterborough Centre for Multicultural Education)
The Infant Assembly Book, *by Doreen Vause* (Macdonald)

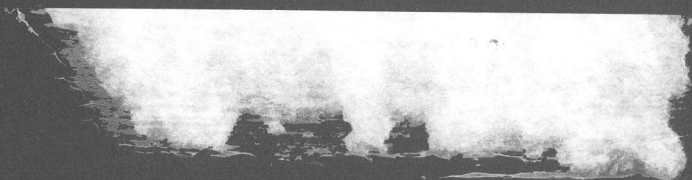